SOGGY
& other first v
by
Mr Joe Bangles

To Mia and Dan

for making a happy man very old

LIMITED FIRST EDITION 200 COPIES

Published by
Witless Productions © 2017
Contact: jlutherh@gmail.com

Soggy Biscuits & other first world problems

ISBN: 978-1-910181-47-8

Published September 2017

Printed and Published by Anchorprint Group Limited
www.anchorprint.co.uk

CONTENTS

Shhh!

I'm making no comment
and claiming
the 5th amendment.
I've got nothing to say
and I won't say it anyway.
I will not yield;
my lips are sealed.
Haven't you heard?
I can't say a word.
I've put a sock in it
and you can
put a clock on it,
because this worm
ain't for turning
and there'll be
no squirming
out of this one.
I'm keeping schtum
and looking after Mum.
I'll mind my
P's & Q's.
I'll put myself
in your shoes.
I've shut my cake hole;
it's the way I roll.
I will not tell.
I will not bleat.
I will not utter.
I will be discrete.
Get it into your head.
Nothing,
no more,
will be said.

THE ROCKET BOYS

Let's build a rocket boys
and blast off to the sun.
I've got some aluminium
and a sticky glue gun.
I want to feel that G-force
slacking back on my cheeks.
Let's go away; not for a day,
but years and months and weeks.

Let's build a rocket boys
and take off to the stars.
All we need is some petrol
and bits from scrapheap cars.
I want to defy gravity,
then spin and flop and flip;
eating food upside down
and bouncing in our starship.

There'll be buttons, knobs and lights
flinging us to far off sights.
Putting flags on purple moons;
chasing cows with wooden spoons.
Boldly going to nowhere
no man has gone before.

Let's build a rocket boys
and fly off into space.
Embracing alien life forms
despite creed, colour or race.
Don't tell your parents fellas,
in an act of ultimate defiance.
Let's build a rocket boys,
it can't be rocket science!

ALPHABETTI SPAGHETTI

My lovely mummy
cooked up for me
a scrummy plate
of Alphabetti Spaghetti
for last night's tea.
On a toasted white
Mother's Pride slice
with melty hot knobs
of buttery blobs
oozing into
an orange splodge
of some sort
of tomato sauce.
I ate a ball
and a bat,
my friend Freddy
and a cat.
X-rays and cars
Jelly Tots and stars.
There were lots of mmmm's
and a number of nnn's.
I made up the word
Fruzzinklytwed!
When my plate was clean
and I was ready for bed,
I made sure I left
an X, Y and Z.

BIG MAN

Big man

is so **big man.**

He **bigger** than me

and **bigger** than you.

He **bigger** than the animals

in Regent Park Zoo.

Big man stand on

the Eiffel Tower.

Big man's eyes

cry April showers.

Big man's shovel hands

dig craters on the moon.

Big man will find you

very *very* soon...

I want to scuff my knees
and climb up trees.
I want to eat cherry lips
and sherbet pips
from a white paper bag,
tied on a piece of string
hanging off the pick n mix
display tray thing,
that has Black Jacks,
Fruit Salads
and flying saucers in.
I want to drink
lager & lime Top Deck
and smoke Old Maid
candy sticks.
Finding my step-dad's
pornographic mags
under the mattress
where he
and my Mum slept.
I want to watch TV
when there were only three
channels.
Spending hours on end
in front of electric bars
that burnt half of my body
and kept the rest of me arctic.
Watching silverfish scuttle
around the red tile hearth.
I want to be Chief Brody
chasing Jaws in the bath,
saving the swimmers of Amity
from a fate worse than death.

I want to read Smash Hits,
the Beano and Scoop
and struggle
to loop the loop
and tie the knot
of the laces
on my new pumps,
that were bought
in Woolworths,
because I had mumps.
I want Christmas
to be a wait forever
and when it comes
……………...it goes,
like it never happened.
I want to score the winner
in a back garden cup final.
Tape the top 40
and listen to vinyl.
I want to not
have the words
when I'm trying
to describe
the thing
I've not felt ,
seen or heard.
I want to get dirty.
I want to be naughty.
I want to be a kid.
I don't want to be forty.

ACROSS THE WATER COOLER

Jesus has been fired.
He turned up late,
it's not the first time.
To be fair,
he had been slacking;
the boss said that
his work was lacking.
Don't say it too loud,
but he'd got in
with the wrong crowd.
Hooked up with
some bloke called Goddy,
that's when his work
became a bit shoddy.
Staying up all the night
saying he'd seen the light;
before he hit the sack.
He went off the tracks.
Started smoking a bit of weed,
well, we all agreed
if he carried on like that
we wouldn't have him back.
So,
Jesus is on his uppers.
Sat at home in his slippers;
watching daytime TV:
Jeremy Kyle, Phillip Schofield
and that Holly Willoughby.
It really is quite sad to see,
we got on well,
him and me,
but he copped off with my bird.
Oh, I thought you'd heard?

Jesus has been retired,
pejoratively speaking.
We kept it quiet,
didn't want it leaking
out to all and sundry.
And now, every Sunday,
I see him busking
along the Strand,
cap in hand,
scraping together
the price of a coffee.
Sometimes, if he's lucky,
he can afford a Cornish pasty,
which beats
baked beans for tea.
He's stuck between a rock
and a hard place.
So, let's say grace
to save his poor soul;
get him out of this hole.
If we get him to confession
he might learn a lesson
or two.
A few bloody Mary's
and some how's your fathers.
Then, on the road to Damascus
and one day he might ask us
for his old job back,
when he's off the crack,
and everything's fine and dandy.
Except, he still gets a bit randy
and can't guarantee
that he won't cop a feel
at the office Christmas party.

Now,
in this company
we like to believe
and we always perceive
to love all creatures
great and small.
However far they fall.
So, deliver him from evil,
lead him not into temptation
and forgive those trespassers
who trespass against him.
Bring him back into the fold
and out of the cold.
Given a second chance,
as long as his enhanced
DBS disclosure
comes back with
no more exposures.
The less said about that the better.
You see,
he is a go-getter
and if he writes
a contrite letter of apology,
we might just be able to see
our way clear
to having him here,
subject to a disciplinary,
in his capacity
as a junior Barista
at the Vatican City
branch of Costa Coffee.

Amen

Ice blue
come to bed   eyes blew
soft skin   me away
lost in   slick back
wet pores   hair black
sweat pours   rose red
lips smack

TEETH

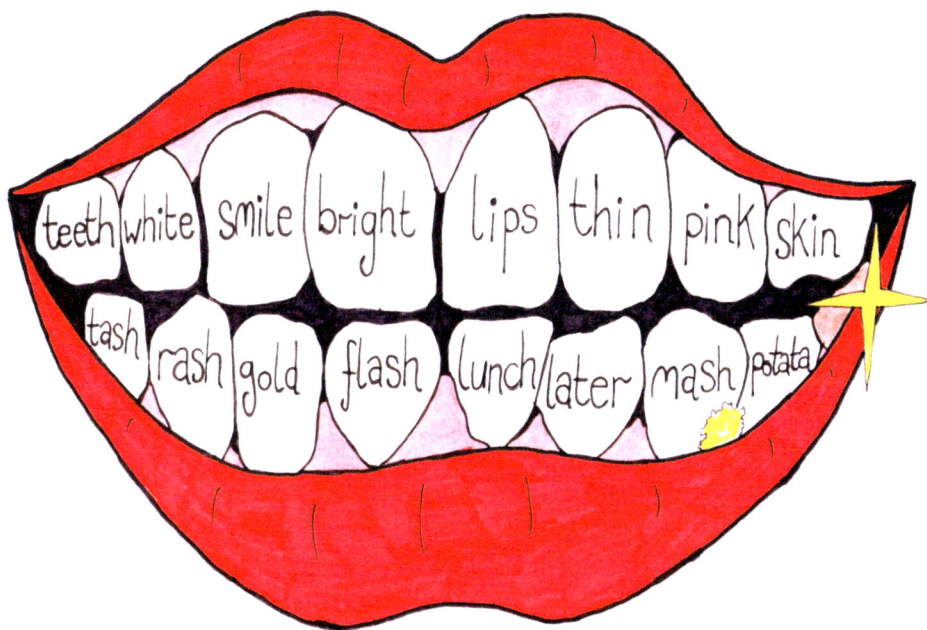

LOOK AT ME

42 mins * 🌐

Look at me
my Facebook friends,
all one thousand
one hundred
and seventy-three
of thee.
Look at me
on Facebook see.
Here I am,
on the beach;
having a barbecue,
drinking tea.
Look at me, look at me.
With some wise words
Confucius said
or maybe it was Katie
Hopkins instead?
Look at me, look at me.
On me holidee;
by the sea
in Tenerife-ee,
taking selfies;
feeling healthy;
looking wealthy,
look at me.
Look at me, look at me
graduating from university,
chucking my mortar
in the air,
getting pissed
at the fresher's fair
and swimming in the sea.

Look at me, look at me.
Striking a yoga pose
with my fake tan
and orange glows;
a sebaceous cyst
on me nose.
Look at me, look at me
drinking Prosecco
in a swanky bar.
I got me a new car
with bull bars
and a tattoo of stars.
One for all
one thousand
one hundred
and seventy-three
of thee.
Look at me.

BIG MAN TOO

...Big man is

too **big man.**

He sit on trees

and lick some clouds.

Big man stand in way.

Big man look over you.

He jump on London

and crush Lord Nelson.

I live on **Big man**

on his **big** eye lid.

You do somewhere too.

Because **Big man**

is so **big man.**

He **bigger** than me

and he **bigger** than you.

I'M GLAD I'M NOT AN ONION

I'm glad I'm not an onion
Wearing an onion sack
Like a green string vest
In a multi-buy pack
With a little white label
Saying Spain, Paraguay
Or somewhere like that

I'm glad I'm not an onion
Making simple folk cry
Spitting caustic acid
In poor people's eyes
I have no hidden layers
What you get is what you see
A funny little tuft of hair
But don't dice with me

I'm glad I'm not an onion
With brittle, fragile skin
A sensitive disposition
And a smile wearing thin
Put me on a chopping board
Slice me down my side
Cut me up and serve me
Steam; sautée or fried

BISCUIT

A chocolate chip cookie,
custard cream
or garibaldi.
Nice or nice?
I never did know.
Desiccated coconut
balls of snow.
Choc and nut crunchies
for teatime munchies,
plain digestives,
fruit jestives
and festives.
Hob-nobbing
with hob nobs
stuffed in your gobs.
Malted milk,
happy cows,
broken bits
cause the rows.
Rich tea;
plain and oblong,
the last one left;
the best one's gone.
Tartan packed shortbread
or ginger snaps instead.
Jaffa cakes
and oatmeal bakes.
Bourbon and custard creams,
lemony puffs; sugary dreams.
Smiley, creamy,
happy faces
munching through
the wacky races.

Jammy dodgers,
yicky, yucky.
Gooey fingers,
sticky, stucky.
Kids in bed,
watching telly,
chomp away,
crumbs on belly.
Mum pigs out
when no-one's in.
Dad sneaks in
and raids the tin.
But the family circle
just drop it out -
"I wanna biscuit"
they all shout.

Personally,
I like to
dunk them in
my cup of tea
or alternatively…

...my coffee.

CAPTAIN FANTASTIC

Champion Cracking Bloody fantastic Super Terrific Going

ballistic Fabulous Brill Fandabidozie Wonderful Marvellous

Life's looking rosy Chipper Topper Tophole to boot Lovely

Mmm...Nice Having a hoot Contented Demented Lapping

it up Ecstatic Emphatic I've got a full cup Pretty darn good

Couldn't be better A Horseshoe Rabbit's foot Luck lady

heather Two magpies Touch wood Round ladders Clean

mirrors Old penny Fresh blood Shiver me timbers Up beat

Down wind Sat on cloud nine Big up High five A wail of a

time Right on Get in Whoop-do-dee-doo Wahey Yee-haw

Scooby-dooby-dooby-doo Excellent Great Time and a half

Alright All set Having a laugh Happy as a sand boy and as

a lark A-grade Distinction Getting top marks Wholesome

Fruitful Glowing with pride Chilling Relaxing Time on my

side Magnificent Majestic Pretty in pink Not blue

Now I feel good.

How about you?

MEMORY

I can forget why
I came in here
in the first place
and what I was
about to say.
I can struggle
for a word
or a phrase.
I can not always recall
just whom
was the second man
to walk on the moon
or who wrote
that ear worm tune.
I can have to go back
to get the bag
that I left on the floor.
Did I remember
to lock the back door
and feed the cat?
I can mislay
my brolly, my gloves
and my hat.
I can be absent-minded
enough to forget
that my specs
are still on my head.
And the specific details
of that little white lie
I said,
which might get me
into trouble
once in a while.

I can have a series
of lists and notes
and reminders.
I can now set the telly
to record Peaky Blinders
because every single time
I forget
that it starts at nine.
I can lose my shirt
my house
and my savings
in a game of cards
because I forgot
that you had
the Queen of Hearts.
I can leave my wallet
on the bar
and my keys
in the ignition
of the car.
But I can't forget
just who you are
and what you
mean to me.

I must never,
ever
forget
my memory.

DUFFED UP

Punched and kicked
Split my lip
Twist and pinched
Bruised my skin
Slapped my face
Stood on my foot
Kicked in the ribs
Pulled my hair
Snapped my wrist
Took a thump
In the solar plexus
Scratched my eyes
Took aim at my flies
That bloody hurt
And made me cry
Now I'm in trouble
Bent over double
A boot to the chin
Capped my knees
A gun to my head
All because of
Something I said
Gave me a shiner
With a right proper
Haymaker
And a neat upper cut
Smashed to a pulp
And duffed up
A total KO
And count to ten
Just to prepare
To beat myself up
Again

FOOT NO SHOE

I've got a foot
without a shoe.
Two broken parts;
ain't got no glue.
One trouser -
no leg.
Hanging out washing
and no clothes peg.
A nice long drink
without a glass.
I can kick a ball,
but can't make a pass.
A cup of tea
with no dunking biscuit.
Sparked electric;
missing a conduit.
A casserole dish
without a stew.
The red letter reminder
when nothing is due.
A sailing ship
without the shore.
I'm stinking rich
when no-one is poor.
I've got an army
with no-one to fight.
I created the universe,
but forgot about light.
I'm a nesting love bird
without a yew tree.
I make a good pair
when you make we.

KALAMANANIMALZOO

KALA-MAN-ANIMAL-ZOO

I saw seagulls in tanktops
and flamingos donning flip flops.
Alligators in fascinators
and crocodiles with mutton chops.
Giraffes had on shower caps
and elephants in their trunks.
Armadillos in stilettos
and chunky woollen tops.
There were sloths in cheesecloth
and penguins dressed in kilts.
Owls in Twhrytt shirts
and lemurs wearing mini-skirts.
I saw a sexy gnu
in thigh-length boots,
giving me the eye,
and a meercat with a bobble hat
eating jelly pie.
Orangutans squeezed into tutus;
tiptoed in their ballet shoes.
The skunks were punks
with mohican cuts
wearing Chanel No. 5.
Mod frogs and rock hoppers
couldn't help but fight with each other,
until the hunky monkeys stepped in.
Then a narwhal wearing an Argyle
came to have a chat,
he said the bats were cats
in their suits and spats,
but the snakes are rats;
bipping their hooters
on their mobility scooters.

Mind you, didn't the hippo
look ever so cute
resplendent in her turtle shell suit?
I had a bit of banter
with a lamb in a tam o' shanter.
There was a gold sequinned macaw
and a tarantula in a fedora
peeping under the door.
I set off to the gift shop
to buy a few presents,
but got distracted by a butterfly
chucking plucked pheasants.
Eventually, when I got to the till
with my anthropological shopping.
I bought a bottle of panda pop
and a razorbill for chopping.
I got some tiger feet shoes
a Nepalese llama snood
and a Spode kangaroo in blue
all on my lovely day out
at the Kalamananimalzoo.

SPACE DUST

One day I won't be here
and I want you to know
that I won't be
overly sad to go.

It's not that I don't love life
or that I don't like you
it's just that there are probably
more interesting things to do.

I reckon I'll be off somewhere,
spinning around,
travelling to places
that have yet to be found.

Exploring the universe
and probably beyond;
floating on winds
and sounds and song.

We're all just space dust
at the end of the day.
I guess that's why
we're made this way.